FANTASTICALLY
faithful
WORLD
CHANGERS
WHO GAVE THEIR ALL FOR GOD

Paul Kerensa is an Award-winning writer of TV, radio, books, and his own stand-up comedy. He is part of the British Comedy award-winning writing team for the BBC's *Miranda* and the Rose d-Or award-winning writing team for BBC1's *Not Going Out*. He's written for shows like BBC's *Top Gear* and Channel 4's *TFI Friday* as well as for BBC Radio 4's *The Now Show* and *Dead Ringers*.

Paul is a regular speaker at Spring Harvest, has toured with the Bible Society, and often does gigs at local churches.

Also in the Fantastically Faithful series:

Fantastically Faithful Heroes
Fantastically Faithful Leaders
Fantastically Faithful Trailblazers

Paul's other books include:

Noah's Car Park Ark
Joe's Bros and the Bus that Goes
Moses and the Exodus Express
Judge Deb and the Battle of the Bands
Planet Protectors! (with Ruth Valerio)
Hark! The Biography of Christmas

PAUL KERENSA

FANTASTICALLY faithful WORLD CHANGERS

WHO GAVE THEIR ALL FOR GOD

STARSHINE B★OKS

Published by **Starshine Books**

Part of the SPCK Group

The Record Hall

16–16A Baldwin's Gardens

London

EC1N 7RJ

www.spck.org.uk

ISBN 978-1-91574-911-6

ebook ISBN 978-1-91574-915-4

Acknowledgements

Scripture quotations are from the ESV Bible (The Holy Bible, English Standard Version), copyright © 2001 by Crossway, a publishing ministry of Good News Publishers. Used by permission. All rights reserved.

Quotations may have been modernised or paraphrased by the author and acknowledgements and copyright notices are provided on p. 108.

First edition 2025

A catalogue record for this book is available from the British Library

Produced on paper from sustainable sources

10 9 8 7 6 5 4 3 2 1

Printed and bound in the UK by Clays Limited

Typeset by Fakenham Prepress Solutions

CONTENTS

FANTASTICALLY FAITHFUL FIRST THOUGHTS

Hello, I'm Paul. I'd like to introduce you to some people who changed the world. Who do you think might be on the list?

After Jesus, the names that leap to my mind (come on, names – leap! leap!) are the famous ones I learned in school. Maybe Isaac Newton, who discovered GRAVITY. The Wright Brothers, who discovered you could DEFY gravity with a plane! How about George Washington, the first US president – who also invented the threshing barn? Or William Shakespeare, who wrote at least 37 plays and came up with the words "amazement" and "majestic" and the phrases "break the ice" and "wild goose chase"?

Well, now I've broken the ice with this wild goose chase (there's no more talk of Shakespeare!), let me tell you why I've invited you into this MAJESTIC book of AMAZEMENT (and yes, you are invited and I'm glad you've accepted the invitation).

We can ALL be world changers.

What an opportunity! We're on this FABULOUS planet to play and dance and eat and chat to people while we eat. And to spot a few injustices or needs, and then to change things for the better. Just as the eight people in this book did.

We'll discover an octet (that means group of eight) of inspirational people, who didn't necessarily set out to change the world – they just did. Each had times of crisis, and often that crisis sent them on a path that led them being a WORLD CHANGER.

They span the world – from Germany to Kenya to Ireland to the United States. They made a difference on the shores of Australia, on the streets of London, and on ships in the Caribbean. They helped street children, prisoners, enslaved people, farm workers, people with disabilities, scared people and worried people . . . and maybe they'll help you, too.

What do you think inspired them to focus on others? I think it was their Christian faith. Their LOVE for Jesus was transformed into action to help others – actions that still benefit people today.

So who are we going to meet, then? And what do we mean by the title *Fantastically Faithful World Changers Who Gave their All for God*?

FANTASTICALLY – Each world changer is simply fantastic, like something out of a fantasy adventure! But their stories are all TRUE . . .

. . . **Like John Newton:** whose life was such an adventure – riding wild waves, telling wild tales, and having a wild time. He was abandoned, enslaved, rescued, then he did the enslaving, then turned against it – mostly while on stormy seas. It's like *Pirates of the Caribbean* meets *Treasure Island* meets . . . well, there are other books on John's bedside table – and one of them's a Bible. Because like the others, he was . . .

FAITHFUL – All of our world changers were full of faith. We'll meet people from different Christian traditions all united by their BELIEF in God.

. . . **Like Joni Eareckson Tada:** whose faith overflows from her and who has changed many people's lives. Her crisis didn't lead to a crisis of faith; instead, her faith is the answer to the crisis. It's almost like she couldn't not respond positively and generously to the situation she found herself in.

If you've read this book once focusing on the main eight people, this time pay attention to the bit parts. You know, the allies, advisors, and cheerleaders who appear only briefly in our world changers' lives, but help them on their way.

From Mariah, the kind woman who found George Washington Carver sitting on a fence, to the person who taught Joni Eareckson Tada to paint with her mouth – these wonderful people were world changers too. They were just the friends that were needed, at just the right time.

WORLD – While each of our superstars set out to help the need they saw in front of them, the repercussions of what they did were felt across the world.

. . . Like Elizabeth Fry: who helped inmates in the prison near where she lived, but when some prisoners were sent to Australia on prison ships, she helped improve their lives on the other side of the planet. Those people went on to change the world where they were, too. So as the world keeps turning, we keep changing it!

CHANGERS – We'll see some great changes in this book: inspiring tales of how situations went from bad to **worse** to better, so much better – often because of one seemingly simple (but oh so complex) decision.

. . . **Like Rosa Parks:** who you could say did something very simple. She sat down and she stayed sitting. She just didn't budge. Can you imagine the energy it takes to not budge? No physical energy, perhaps, but wow – the emotional energy, the mental strength, the spiritual va-va-voom . . . Rosa had this in spades, and her decision to use it changed her life, and the lives of her people, and her city, and her country, and . . . you get the idea. It's probably changed other planets somehow – I just don't know how yet.

WHO – As well as getting to know their impact on the world, we'll get to know who these people were. And how their "who" shaped their "what", "when", and "how". (There's generally a "why" in there somewhere, too.)

. . . **Like Wangarĩ Maathai:** who we get to know by finding out about her childhood and student life. She never forgot where she came from, who she grew up with, and how she could use her skills to help them. How generous! Which brings us to . . .

GAVE – Each of our world changers was more concerned with what they could do for others than what others could do for them.

. . . **Like Christian Führer:** who submitted his life to God, serving as a priest, and gave his time and energy in pursuit of PEACE and HOPE. But giving hope was almost revolutionary in East Germany at the time. Sending out messages of peace risked being met with violence. But he kept on giving, especially every Monday evening (as you'll see) for decades.

THEIR – These world changers used the gifts God had given them: their unique skills in their unique circumstances. It feels like nobody else could have achieved the same thing in the way that these eight did. Just as you are the only you, each one of them was their own person and EXACTLY who God wanted them to be.

. . . **Like George Washington Carver**: whose enthusiasm for education and agriculture set him on a unique course through life. From his early days when he was enslaved and kidnapped, to his love of learning, to his determination to help poor farmers . . . and somehow all of this led to a lot of peanuts!

ALL – These world changers gave their all. They didn't work nine to five then clock off. "World changer" isn't a job you advertise online! Their brilliantly impactful actions really only had the effect they had because they each gave EVERYTHING of themselves . . .

. . . **Like Thomas Barnardo:** who could have done great things as a medical student, studying and working by day. But by keeping his eyes open, he spotted problems that needed fixing. Even alert in the middle of the night, walking in the middle of London, his QUEST to look after the city's street children took all his time and focus. His schools and children's homes came about because he gave his all.

FOR GOD – Each of our world changers had an ultimate goal: to GLORIFY God. God made the world, and he made us. But the world went **wrong**. So perhaps we can do what we can to change it? Isn't that what its creator would want?

So if you'd like to change the world for the better, be you, be AWESOME, be generous, and be the BEST version of you there can be – that's God's plan for you.

To help with this, at the end of each chapter, there are a few questions for you to think about, a short Bible passage to read, and a prayer to bring everything together before God.

Now, let's get INSPIRED by these eight fantastically faithful world changers . . .

CHAPTER 1

JOHN NEWTON

(1725–1807)

What do you think is the world's **BIGGEST** problem? Imagine if you were part of the problem for years and years – could you then be part of the solution to fix it? (Oh, then imagine going on to write one of the most famous songs in the history of the world! Amazing . . .)

This is the story of John Newton: a British sea captain who went from slave trader to slave trade abolisher. He came to know that despite the many mistakes he made in his life, God would still offer him his AMAZING gift of grace.

It's also a story about a ship, a book, and some hymns. Oh yes, he did a lot of sailing and a lot of singing. It wasn't all hymns in church – there were quite a few sea shanties, too . . .

John was born in 1725 in Wapping, East London, near the docks where ships left the River Thames for every major port in the world. London was a hub of maritime mayhem. At a time when exploration, trade, and sometimes conflict at sea were all **BIG** business, the city was riding the crest of a wave.

So if you need ships, who do you need to make them? Shipbuilders! Like John's father (also called John). As for John's mother Elizabeth, she sadly wasn't well, and died of an illness that was common then – tuberculosis – when John was just six years old. She had raised John in the Christian faith, but very quickly he forgot about it.

John was sent away by his dad and new stepmother, first to boarding school, then to sea. He spent his teenage years on ships, often with his dad. He joined the Royal Navy aged 18, on the HMS *Harwich*.

But John wasn't exactly a model sailor. He was wild! He *drank* too much, made up **rude** songs, and generally misbehaved. His captain punished him in front of the crew, flogging him with a whip, and demoting him to a lower rank – but it only made John misbehave more. So when the captain had **REALLY** had enough of him, John was transferred to the *Pegasus* – a ship heading to West Africa as part of the slave trade.

Slavery has existed for thousands of years. You may have read the story in the Bible of Moses freeing enslaved Israelites from the wicked Pharaoh.

There was almost no slavery in Europe in the 1400s, but in the 1500s ships and seafaring took off in a whole new way (well, they didn't "take off" – flying ships would come a lot later).

Britain, Holland, Portugal, Spain, and others began colonizing countries on the other side of the Atlantic. They wanted people to work there, but didn't want to pay them. This led to the Atlantic Slave Trade.

A ship would leave Europe loaded with goods, like brandy and guns, and sail to West Africa, where the goods were sold and African people – often kidnapped – were "bought". These people were then taken in horrific conditions to new colonies in the Americas, where they were "sold" as slaves. The ship filled up with more goods, like cotton and sugar, which were taken back to Europe to sell, and the whole terrible triangle began again.

For 300 years, this trade route treated people as goods. It was too big a system to just stop, with too many rich and powerful people involved in it. It needed many brave and determined people to help end it . . .

John did not change his ways. His new crew were just as annoyed by his general naughtiness. Would nobody like his rude songs? NO! Stop singing, John!

The crew hatched a plan to get rid of him. Their whole trade was about swapping goods for people, to enslave them. Why not do the same with John?

So 20-year-old John became another item to be swapped and traded. He was left on the African coast with a slave trader called Amos Clowe, who enslaved John and gave him to his wife, Princess Peye. She treated him TERRIBLY, starving him and encouraging others to throw garbage at him. John wasn't singing so much now . . .

Though enslaved, John had something others didn't – an influential father who could rescue him. So when word of his fate reached John Newton Senior, seafarers on the West African coast were asked to look out for this ne'er-do-well. (Don't know this word? It literally means "never-do-well". As in someone who never does well. Like John. Although some of his songs were quite catchy.)

As the only white person for miles, John Junior was easy to find. After three years of slavery, he was heading HOME on yet another ship: the *Greyhound*. But he swiftly went back to his old habits of drinking heavily, mocking Christians, and singing rude songs. Yet this voyage home would bring a change of weather – and a change of FAITH.

Onboard John read a book called *The Imitation of Christ*. "Be like Christ?" he wondered. How could he do that, after the wretched life he'd led? Then came the storm.

In March 1748, just off the Irish coast, fierce gales rocked the *Greyhound*. A hole was RIPPED in its side, and several sailors were lost to the waves. In this moment of crisis, John had a few small words of prayer: "Lord, have mercy on us."

He shocked himself by saying those words, later admitting, "This was the first desire I had breathed for mercy for many years!"

The storm calmed and John was SAVED. By the time he reached Britain, John decided to trust in God. But he didn't immediately change his ways. The storm was a turning-point; he gave up gambling, drinking, and bad language – but he had a LONG way to go.

For the next ten years, John continued to make money from the slave trade, going from ship to ship, port to port, job to job, earning and learning (slowly) the mistakes of his past.

As he read the Bible and prayed, he began to realize that he couldn't save his soul by trying, and then failing, to improve. He couldn't earn his salvation. Only God could save him, and this underserved GIFT OF GRACE was amazing! Hmm, there might be a song in that . . .

John did become a FULL believer and, at the age of 33, he felt called to be a priest. It took five years, but eventually he was ordained a priest in the Church of England. His church leadership style was all about sharing his story of being SAVED, using his skills of writing, preaching, and music. His congregation grew.

Those wild, rude songs he wrote at sea were all training for hymn-writing! For a while John wrote one new hymn each week, linking with his sermons. In 1772, in his late 40s, he came up with a belter. To communicate God's amazing grace, John wrote . . . er, well, "Amazing Grace". It told his own tale: being a lowly wretch, lost then found, finding God's PROMISE and PROTECTION. There was even a "bright shining . . . sun", just like the African sun that he had toiled under. It's become one of the BEST-LoVED hymns in the world.

John's experiences at sea stayed with him – and fuelled the most world-changing chapter in his life. When he moved to a London church, he became more involved in politics and protest. He began campaigning against the slave trade that was such a HUGE part of his earlier life.

John's major achievement came at the age of 60, when up-and-coming politician William Wilberforce came knocking at his door . . . literally. William had grown up Christian, but drifted from his faith – just like John had from his childhood faith – and now wanted to go back. William was uncertain, though, about how to mix faith and politics. Should he stop being a politician? Become a priest like John? John said no! Stay in politics, do God's work there. Make change happen at the heart of government.

So William did. Encouraged by John, he shone a light on the horrors of the slave trade. Their friendship bridged the worlds of protesting priests (who were anti-slavery but didn't have any power to stop it) and politicians (who could change things but didn't always want to). Together, in 1787, they formed the Anti-Slavery Society. A year later, John published a pamphlet called *Thoughts Upon the African Slave Trade*, which described the terrible

conditions that enslaved people suffered when they were transported. He had copies sent to **ALL** the politicians and it became very influential in the fight against slavery.

For the next 19 years, John campaigned with William to abolish slavery. He was full of **regret** and **sadness** that he had once played a part in the terrible trade in human lives and did EVERYTHING he could to bring it to an end.

Change came slowly: so many powerful people profited from slavery that it wasn't until 1807 that a law passed

Not all Christians were on the right side of the fight against slavery. The Church, and some church members, made a lot of money from slavery. They justified this horrific practice by saying that it was part of God's plan, and that Paul had instructed slaves to obey their masters (e.g. Ephesians 6:5). They didn't want to change a system that they benefited from.

Thankfully, other Christians understood that God created all people equal. Many leading abolitionists (those who worked to abolish slavery) were motivated by their faith to bring about an end to the terrible idea that one person can "own" another.

making the slave trade illegal in Britain and the British Empire. John died just nine months later, his life's work COMPLETE.

It would take a further 58 years, and a war, for slavery to FINALLY be abolished in the United States, but that's another story.

John's faith had veered like a ship in a storm. He'd worked in the scorching sun and survived wild wind and rain on the *Greyhound*'s deck. From faithless to SUPER-FAITHFUL, he'd been a slave trader and then fought to stop it all. Above all, despite everything he had done, thought, said, and sung, John knew that God still LOVED him and wanted to use him to change the world. And God did. So John did.

"AMAZING GRACE! (HOW SWEET THE SOUND) THAT SAVED A WRETCH LIKE ME! I ONCE WAS LOST, BUT NOW AM FOUND, WAS BLIND, BUT NOW I SEE."

JOHN NEWTON

THINK

- John grew to regret his part in the slave trade. Think of a time when you treated someone unkindly. What could you do differently next time?

- Listen to a recording of the song "Amazing Grace", or perhaps look up the lyrics. What does God's grace mean to you? (If you need a reminder of what "grace" means, see p. 13.)

READ

For by grace you have been saved through faith. And this is not your own doing; it is the gift of God, not a result of works, so that no one may boast.

Ephesians 2:8–9

PRAY

Loving Father,

Thank you for the life of John Newton. Thank you that there is nothing we can say or do (or sing!) that will stop you loving us, because of your amazing grace. Through whatever storms lie ahead in our lives, be with us, as you were with John. Help us to do what's right, to be kind to one another, and to change the world for the better – even if it takes a lifetime.

Amen.

CHAPTER 2

ELIZABETH FRY

(1780–1845)

Where do you begin changing the world? Start at the TOP, with kings, queens, presidents, and prime ministers? Or try to improve things for those in the middle, in regular houses with regular jobs? Or begin caring for those who can't help themselves, because they're stuck, in one room, in prison, in the worst conditions?

This is the story of Elizabeth Fry: a British woman who became a social reformer after a prison visit opened her eyes to life inside. She improved conditions behind bars so much – especially for female inmates – that she was called "the ANGEL of Prisons". (That doesn't mean she helped break people out – she wasn't that sort of angel . . .)

It's also a story about some iron bars, a food basket, and paper money. (Now, depending on when you read this, you might need me to explain what "paper" money is. Before card payments, we used to pay for things in cash. This was coins and paper things – you know, notes or bills. Elizabeth Fry appeared on one. We'll get to that. First, we head to prison. Well, no, actually *first* we head to the bank . . .)

Before she was a Fry, Elizabeth Gurney was born in 1780 in Norwich in the east of England, to a banking family. Her father, John Gurney, had a family business – Gurney's Bank – while her mother, Catherine, was part of the Barclay family, who **ALSO** had a bank! Long after Elizabeth's life, both family banks merged (with other banks) to form Barclays Bank, *still* one of the world's biggest banks today.

As if that wasn't enough family business, Elizabeth married Joseph Fry of the Fry family, whose chocolate company gave us the first **MASS-PRODUCED** chocolate bar. J. S. Fry & Son Limited, set up by Joseph's uncle, was famous for the popular Fry's Turkish Delight and the world's first hollow chocolate Easter egg. **Yum!**

But more important than her famous families were her **FRIENDS**, or I should say her Friends. The Gurneys and Frys were all Quakers, also known as the Religious Society of Friends. As the name suggests, Quakers are friendly people who believe it's important to LISTEN to God and act as he wishes, to treat everyone as equals, and to speak the truth. Quaker meetings are often silent, or at least very quiet, to be attentive for God's word.

Elizabeth felt a divine urge to help others. In 1813, soon after having her eighth child (she had 11 in total!), she visited London's Newgate Prison, to see how prisoners lived and see if she could help. But she was SHOCKED at what she saw.

Prisoners were kept in cramped conditions, in rooms built for 60 people but housing 300. There weren't enough beds for the prisoners, so many slept on straw. People cooked bad food in their cells, where they also washed and used the toilet . . . except there was no toilet, just a corner.

Many people were locked away, forgotten, and not given proper treatment. For some it was their last stop in Britain before boarding prison ships for Australia.

Elizabeth's focus was especially on women and children. Yes, CHILDREN were locked up too! A child might be sentenced to prison for something as little as stealing a loaf of bread, or because their mother had committed a crime.

A typical situation might look like this: a DESPERATE family might be starving, so the mother might steal an apple at the market. She'd then be arrested and sent to prison, without trial. If the father was still around (if he hadn't abandoned them or died), he'd still be out working to earn money, so any children would be imprisoned with their mother, and they might be headed for Australia on one of those prison ships! So often, this was simply because a mother wanted to give her children some food . . . and those market apples looked so tempting.

In 1787, to reduce London's overcrowding and a prison system bursting at the seams, 11 ships left Britain for Australia – just over half of them packed with convicts.

Before that, prisoners had been sent to the Americas but after Britain lost the American War of Independence, this new destination was chosen far across the world. The place was actually selected by Lord Sandwich . . . inventor of the sandwich!

But their epic voyage was no picnic. There weren't enough sandwiches for these convicts, or enough other food for that matter. Many arrived in Australia starving. They were plagued by bedbugs, fleas, dehydration, and sickness. Their punishment continued in this new land, breaking rocks, and their backs, as they built new roads.

Despite these terrible conditions, the prison ships continued until the 1860s when they were abolished, partly thanks to Elizabeth Fry.

Even before boarding those boats, Newgate Prison had similarly awful accommodation, as Elizabeth had spotted . . .

The system's unfairness was not something Elizabeth could easily OVERTURN, but she could provide food and clothing for the poor inmates at Newgate.

So the day after her first visit, Elizabeth returned to the prison with whatever she could fit in a basket. She followed Jesus' example to FEED and CLOTHE those in need.

In 1816, she raised funds for a new school . . . inside the prison. This meant that imprisoned children could learn, and have a chance at a BETTER future. She ensured

the prisoners themselves got to decide what was fair in the school. She suggested some rules and the prisoners voted on them. It gave them some control, when everything around them felt so out of control.

With the school up and running, Elizabeth turned her attention to the women. How could they develop SKILLS for when they left prison? By bringing in materials and needles and teaching them to sew, Elizabeth gave them greater job opportunities . . . plus they had a fun hobby to pass the time in prison.

Elizabeth needed help to spread her ideas beyond Newgate: she needed the support of rich and influential people as well as politicians and charity campaigners. Elizabeth encouraged and arranged for them to visit Newgate Prison, to witness the appalling conditions, and to see the improvements she was making.

Elizabeth's ideas gradually helped change the idea of what prison was all about. Most thought people in prison deserved to be there because they were lazy and immoral, and that prisons should be places of punishment to teach them a lesson. But Elizabeth thought prison should help improve lives, teaching LOTS of lessons, from needlework to cookery. Elizabeth said, "Punishment is not for revenge, but to lessen crime and REFORM the criminal."

In 1818 Elizabeth was invited to present her findings to the British government. She was the first woman **EVER** to do this! Her evidence led to the passing of the Gaols Act of 1823 and the Prisons Act of 1835. ("Gaol" is just a different spelling for "jail" but it means and sounds the same!) From then on, female prisoners were separated from male prisoners, and inspectors checked that conditions were as decent as possible.

Elizabeth also visited the convict ships sailing to Australia, ensuring there was EDUCATION for the children, sewing materials for the women (so that they had something to sell when they arrived), food for all . . . and Bibles, too! She also campaigned for better conditions for women already transported to Australia.

What had begun in Newgate spread to other prisons, and Elizabeth visited other countries in Europe to talk about prison conditions and sparked reform there, too. Her work improved life not just for the **THOUSANDS** of people in prison in her time, but also for those who have found themselves in prison since. World changing!

Elizabeth's faith was at the heart of everything she did. She was a big believer in putting God's plans into ACTION: to show divine love by helping others. The changes she made were so **HUGE** that in 2002, this daughter of bankers had her face printed on British paper money – the £5 note bore Elizabeth's face for the next 15 years. Her banking parents would have been so PROUD!

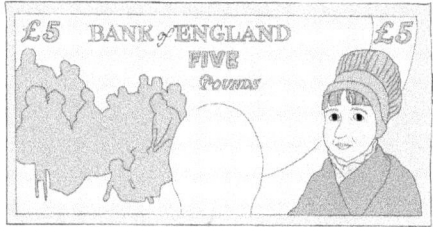

"IF THE WORK BE
AS I TRUST IT IS, OF
THE LORD, IT WILL GO
ON WITHOUT A POOR
CREATURE LIKE ME."

ELIZABETH FRY

THINK

- Grab a piece of paper and some pens and design some money with your face on it! Now add "For services to . . ." what? What might you do to earn your place on a bank note?

- Jesus came for everyone, and no one is beyond his love. Think of someone whom you struggle to like, and then spend a moment thinking about them as a child of God, whom Jesus loves – just like you!

READ

For the LORD hears the needy
and does not despise his own people who are prisoners.

Psalm 69:33

PRAY

God of all,

Thank you for the life and work of Elizabeth Fry. Thank you for the difference she made changing lives across the world, from the prisons of London to the shores of Australia. Bless people in prison across the world today, may they know your love and peace. Bless those who have been hurt by crime, may they know your healing love. Help us to remember that Jesus came to save us all and that no one is beyond your reach.

Amen.

CHAPTER 3

THOMAS BARNARDO
(1845–1905)

What do you do if you see a **great** need? Someone needs something – maybe a meal, or a toy, or a friend? What if you met a child without a school, or even a home? What if you met **THOUSANDS** of such children? Do you walk on by? Or start building?

This is the story of Thomas John Barnardo: an Irish medical student who saw a problem . . . and fixed it. He dedicated his life to providing education and homes for thousands of children. He didn't just build a **house**, he built a **village**!

It's also a story about a school, some shiny shoes, and a toy bear. He's called Barney. Do you have a cuddly toy? (I have a rabbit called Bun-Buns, but don't **tell** my grown-up friends, because they don't know.)

Thomas was born in 1845 in Dublin, Ireland, but his family were from all sorts of places. Thomas's father, John, was German, from a Spanish–Jewish family with probably an Italian surname! Thomas's mother, Abigail, was English, part of a Christian community called the Plymouth Brethren, who believed in "the Bible alone".

Thomas learned about Christianity through his childhood, then aged 16 he decided for himself that God was REAL and that Christ was the one to FOLLOW . . . and that others should know about him, too. He began preaching in Dublin but quickly set his sights across the world. He planned to go to China as a missionary, where his mission would be to tell people about Jesus. To get there – and to offer physical as well as spiritual help – he went to London to train at medical school. He would be a missionary and a doctor.

But after two years studying, something bothered him. Countless children in London's East End, the poorest parts of the city, were missing out on an education. At the time, education was not compulsory and only children from wealthy families went to school. So Thomas refocused his mission; not on China, but on London's street children. Thomas had the money, so in 1868 he opened a school.

Thomas established a place of HOPE on a street called Hope Place. It was called the East End Juvenile Mission, one of several "ragged schools" that gave some of the poorest children somewhere SAFE to learn and the hope of a better future. But this was just the start . . .

One boy in particular made an **impact** on Thomas: ten-year-old Jim Jarvis.

At the end of one school day, when the other children left, young Jim stayed by the fireside. "Time to go home!" said Thomas, but Jim had **no** home, mother or father. His latest bed was a hay-cart by a market, but he'd spent years moving around, trying to stay out of trouble on London's **dangerous** streets.

"I looked at the little lad whom I now know the Lord had sent me," Thomas wrote, "and could not but see how

These free schools were named after the children living in poverty who needed them – those whose appearance was "ragged", often literally, with little more than rags to wear and no possessions.

Ragged schools appeared in the early 1800s, mostly in London but also in Scotland, and always in poorer areas. Most were set up by individual Christians wanting to make a difference. Pupils were fed and educated, perhaps learning skills like carpentry or cookery.

One early supporter of ragged schools was the author Charles Dickens. After visiting the Field Lane Ragged School, he was inspired to write a story about a poor child called Tiny Tim. If you haven't heard of *A Christmas Carol*, then . . . bah, humbug!

ill-prepared he was to resist the inclement weather." In other words, it was freezing cold and Jim was dressed in nothing but rags!

Thomas PRAYED for Jim, then asked if there were other children who were similarly desperate. "More 'n I could count," Jim replied, immediately leading Thomas on a tour of London to see where other children slept. They scaled walls and entered gl00my sheds before finding boys aged from 9 to 18, sleeping on a rooftop.

Soon after, Thomas attended a missionaries meeting and spoke about child homelessness. He enthused others, who returned to the streets with him to find children sleeping in crates, under tarpaulin sheets, and behind barrels. Many children were afraid to come out, but emerged when they saw bread and sausages waiting for them!

Thomas decided then that the ragged school wasn't enough and he set up a home for 25 orphaned boys.

As well as being taught to read and write, the boys were given Bible classes and taught other life skills. One of these skills was shoe-shining. This gave them a much-needed job: brightening the footwear of London's middle and upper classes. Other lads became newsboys, fetching and carrying the daily newspapers. By the time Thomas's young guests left the home, they were employable. They had a FUTURE.

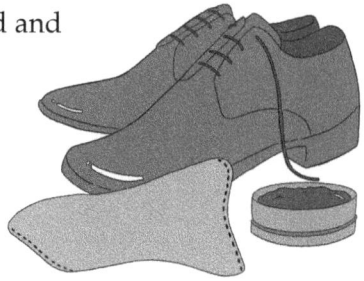

Thomas wanted to know what had caused the children to lose so much, so he asked them. A HUGE amount – 85% – said that alcohol had played a big part. It was too cheap, too easy to get, and too disruptive to family life. So Thomas stopped drinking alcohol, and began actively preaching against it. He held mission meetings outside pubs and bars, making lots of enemies among those who ran the venues or liked drinking there. Thomas preferred to preach not in churches, but out and about . . . even if he was pelted with rotten fruit by the pub-goers!

Back at his children's home, the beds were full, so when one boy knocked on the door, Thomas reluctantly turned him away. Sadly, the boy didn't last more than a few days in the London winter, so Thomas resolved NEVER to turn anyone away. He put up a sign outside: "No Destitute Boy Ever Refused Admission".

That meant building new homes! When, sometime later, a young girl knocked on the door and asked if they took girls too, the sign was changed to "No Destitute Child Ever Refused Admission". Thomas founded the Girls' Village Home, which was actually many homes, housing 1,500 girls! One cottage was just for babies, another cared for ill children, and there were also dressmaking and embroidery schools . . . the village even had its own church.

Thomas challenged the opinions of most people at the time, who thought poverty was a result of laziness and wickedness. He believed that ALL children are loved by God and he accepted all children into his homes, regardless of why they were poor, what their abilities were, and what ethnicity they were.

In time, over 120 orphanages could fit 8,500 children. Ultimately around 60,000 children passed through "Dr Barnardo's Homes". Thomas campaigned against child poverty and wrote nearly 200 books on the subject. He never finished medical school, but was later awarded a doctorate anyway. His title of Dr Barnardo was WELL-EARNED!

Thomas died in 1905, but the Barnardo's charity continues today, focusing on fostering and adoption. This is something that Thomas himself began to model. From 1887, he was "boarding out" children, finding FAMILY homes to care for them, rather than keeping them in orphanages. The Barnardo's mascot, Barney the Bear, is a reminder that EVERY child matters, every child needs to feel safe, and every child needs a FRIEND . . . a friend like the one London's street children found in Thomas.

Thomas's plans changed through his life, from preaching in Dublin, to his planned mission to China, to responding to the great need found in his own streets. He changed the world by TRANSFORMING tens of thousands of lives, sending young people out to be world changers of their own!

"I HOPE TO DIE AS I
HAVE LIVED, IN THE
HUMBLE BUT ASSURED
FAITH OF JESUS CHRIST
AS MY SAVIOUR, MY
MASTER AND MY KING."

THOMAS BARNARDO

THINK

- Thomas really listened to the children he was helping. Why is it important for grown-ups to listen to kids? What might the grown-ups learn?

- Next time you see someone who needs help, see if you can listen to God: what would he want you to do?

READ

But Jesus called them to him, saying, "Let the children come to me, and do not hinder them, for to such belongs the kingdom of God."

Luke 18:16

PRAY

Loving Father,

Thank you for the life and service of Thomas Barnardo. Help us to see the needs of others, to ask the right questions, and to listen to the answers so that we may respond to your call to make your world a better place. Thank you for all those who look after children in foster care. Bless all children who live in care and give them a brighter future.

Amen.

CHAPTER 4

GEORGE WASHINGTON CARVER

(ABOUT 1864-1943)

If you make a discovery, or come up with an invention, or have a great idea, do you take all the GLORY? Do you keep the idea for yourself to make a heap of money? Or do you SHARE your idea freely? Our next world changer understood that God was working through him, so everything he discovered belonged to all God's children.

This is the story of George Washington Carver: an African American farmer, scientist, inventor, and educator. He began his earthly life enslaved. He ended his earthly life with numerous awards and titles . . .
and peanuts.

It's also a story about a barn, or even two, some yummy scrummy peanuts, and a wagon. Did we

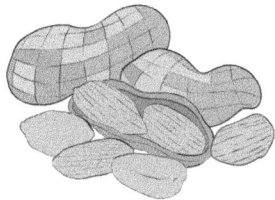

mention peanuts? There are LOTS of peanuts. George Washington Carver is The Peanut Man (that was literally his nickname!).

George was born in Newton County, Missouri, in . . . well, it's tricky to know when. He was born into an enslaved family, so there wasn't a record of his birth. It was just before slavery was outlawed in 1865, so let's say it was 1864 . . . -ish.

When he was born, George was simply given the name "George" – both the "Washington" and the "Carver" came later.

George's family were enslaved by landowners Moses and Susan Carver. His father died before George was born and then, when George was just one week old, he, his mother, and his sister were kidnapped! Moses tracked down the kidnappers, who were taking enslaved people to "resell" them, and baby George was brought home. His mother and sister were not – they had been sold on.

Slavery was abolished and Moses and Susan raised George and his older brother James as part of their family. George and James were not allowed to go to church because it was ONLY for white people. One day when working in the barn, and inspired by a conversation about Sunday school with a young white boy, George knelt and

PRAYED. It was then that, in his words, "God just came into my heart".

The Carvers taught George how to read and write and encouraged him to get as good an education as possible . . . but that wasn't easy. And so began George's lifelong love of – and battle to get – education.

Most schools didn't admit black children, so the nearest school open to him was TEN miles away. George set off, but by the time that 14-year-old George got there, it was not open because it was night-time!

One thing that was open was a barn door, so George entered and **slept** there for the night. Yawn! Next morning, he awoke from his bed of hay and perched outside on the fence. Passing by was a KIND woman, Mariah Watkins, also formerly enslaved. When Mariah asked George who he was, he replied "Carver's George" as if he were still enslaved. Mariah told him that from now on, he was to be George Carver.

On the plantation where Mariah had lived, only one person knew how to read: a woman called Libby. Enslaved people were **BANNED** from reading in case it gave them ideas about freedom, but Libby had **secretly** taught others how to read. Mariah knew how important it was that George gained this SKILL and made the most of it. To help with this, she offered him a room to rent, near the school. She also gave him a Bible.

"You must learn all you can," Mariah told George. "Then be like Libby. Go out into the world and GIVE your learning back to our people. They're starving for a little learning!" That message sums up George's entire life.

Now I know what you're thinking. This is all very well, but where are the peanuts? Alright, alright, they're coming. Peanuts take time to grow, as George could have told you. George learned a LOT about agriculture, how and when crops grow, and how patient you need to be. And throughout his education, George had to be very patient.

He was a hard worker, doing jobs far and wide outside of his school hours. He was gifted at science, especially botany (the study of plants), so he applied to colleges. He was accepted by a college in Kansas, but just like his first day at school, he arrived to find it closed . . . at least, closed to him. It was not clear on his college application that he was black, and so when the college saw him in person, they REFUSED to admit him. Slavery may have been over, but George was faced with the racist education system that followed it.

So George kept working hard in nearby towns, putting his agricultural learning into action. He planted all sorts of crops from fruit trees to rice to corn. Still eager to learn, he moved to Iowa and in 1890 began studying art and music. He put his LOVE of nature into his artwork, depicting his favourite plants and flowers. George once said: "I love to think of NATURE as unlimited broadcasting stations, through which God speaks to us every day, every hour and every moment of our lives, if we will only tune in."

There was more education ahead, too. His art teacher's father was a professor at Iowa State Agricultural College, and before long George became the FIRST black student to enrol at what is now Iowa State University. There was another George Carver at the university, and the mail kept getting mixed up, so our George added the middle name "Washington". He also added some letters after his name, gaining both his first degree, and then a second degree, earning him the title "Master of Science". He became the university's first black teacher and his research gained RESPECT across the country.

There was yet another move to another state, when George was asked to head up the agricultural department at Alabama's Tuskegee Institute . . . which he led for the next 47 years!

During his time teaching, George set up a Bible study class each Sunday evening, beginning with seven students but soon over a HUNDRED regularly came to hear George's thoughts on creation and the creator.

Now one of the country's greatest EXPERTS in agriculture, George developed all sorts of farming techniques. Crop rotation meant growing different crops in the same ground at different times, helping different nutrients boost each crop. This included the humble peanut . . .

Peanuts were an ideal crop for farmers without much land, who were struggling to make money. They were easy and cheap to grow. But there wasn't much demand for them.

George studied peanuts from 1903, and in 1920 presented "The Possibilities of the Peanut". How many uses can you think of for peanuts? George thought of HUNDREDS!

George never forgot the importance of passing his education onto others. As well as growing crops, he was keen to grow the character of his students.

He came up with "eight cardinal virtues" to help them reach their full potential:

1. Be clean both inside and out.

2. Neither look up to the rich or down on the poor.

3. Lose, if need be, without squealing.

4. Win without bragging.

5. Always be considerate of women, children, and older people.

6. Be too brave to lie.

7. Be too generous to cheat.

8. Take your share of the world and let others take theirs.

George gave this advice over 100 years ago, but it's still good for today!

Shampoo, shaving cream, glue, axle grease . . . Oh, and you could **eat** them. George came up with **105** different recipes, from peanut cookies to peanut sausages! Now everyone was demanding peanuts, and farmers had something **PROFITABLE** and nutritious to grow.

George also loved sweet potatoes, which could be eaten but also used to make, among other things, shoe polish and soap. George said that **peanuts** and **sweet potatoes** were "two of the greatest products that God has ever given us".

George was PASSIONATE about sharing this knowledge to farmers, which meant hitting the road. A wealthy banker, Morris Ketchum Jesup, wanted to support George's great work so he donated money so that George could afford to develop a mobile classroom.

From 1906, the "Jesup wagon" toured around teaching farmers how to grow crops. First it was a horse-drawn cart, then later it upgraded to a truck. Modern versions are STILL in use today!

Many scientists and inventors patent their creations, which means no one else can copy them and make money from them, but George patented hardly any of his. He preferred to SHARE his inventions with others, especially African American farmers. His gravestone has an inscription: "He could have added fortune to fame, but caring for neither, he found happiness and honor in being HELPFUL to the world."

From his birth, enslaved and kidnapped, to his longing for education and his EAGERNESS to spread knowledge like he was scattering seeds, George had quite a life. He battled against discrimination to make AMAZING

51

DISCOVERIES that continue to help farmers today. He was known across the country for campaigning against racism, sharing his faith . . . and promoting peanuts!

"LOVE IS MORE POWERFUL THAN HATE."

GEORGE WASHINGTON CARVER

THINK

- George was passionate about the science of farming and he couldn't wait to share what he knew with others. What hobby or interest would you love to share with others? Why do you like it so much?

- George saw God's work in nature. Spend some time in nature thinking about the wonder of God's creation. Even something as simple as a flower can show you his awesome craftsmanship!

READ

"Worthy are you, our Lord and God,
   to receive glory and honour and power,
for you created all things,
   and by your will they existed and were created."

   Revelation 4:11

PRAY

Creator God,

We praise you for your incredible creation. Thank you for crops that grow and the people who grow them. Thank you for George Washington Carver, for his love of learning and his eagerness to share his knowledge to help others. Give us curiosity to learn new things, the confidence to share our knowledge with others, and a passion to tell others of your love.

Amen.

CHAPTER 5

ROSA PARKS

(1913–2005)

Wouldn't it be a topsy-turvy world if sometimes to stand **UP** you have to sit **down**? But isn't it a topsy-turvy world if some people are thought to be better than others, and given more rights just because of the way they look? Could you bravely be the ONE person standing up (or sitting down) in a room-ful – or bus-ful – of opposition?

This is the story of Rosa Parks: an African American seamstress who campaigned for equal rights for black people and became known as the mother of the civil rights movement. She took the most famous bus ride of all time.

It's also a story about a bus token (like a bus ticket), a seat, and $14. It may be a story you've heard before, but I'm sure you'll find out some things you don't already know. For example, did you know that Rosa was born in the same city that George Washington Carver (from the last chapter) was teaching in? (See his chapter to discover where . . . or read the next line!)

Rosa Louise McCauley was born in 1913 in Tuskegee, Alabama. When she was two, she and her mother moved to her grandparents' house near Montgomery, the state capital of Alabama. The family read the Bible and prayed every day, and Rosa learned to TRUST God.

Although slavery was abolished, prejudice and segregation remained in many southern states. Black and white people had separate places to learn, shop, worship, and work. Rosa's school was for black children, but the buses on the road to school were mostly full of white people so Rosa and her friends had to walk there.

Life was difficult and frightening, but Rosa had become used to it. Rosa later said, "The bus was among the first ways I realized there was a black world and a white world."

In 1932, Rosa married Raymond Parks, a member of the National Association for the Advancement of Colored People (NAACP). Ten years later, Rosa began working as a secretary for the civil rights movement. But the couple had day jobs, too: he was a barber, she was a seamstress in a shirt factory.

In 1943, Rosa paid for a token and boarded a bus, but the driver, James F. Blake, told her to use the rear doors. When she obeyed, he drove off

LEAVING her by the roadside. She never forgot Blake's face, and vowed never to board a bus if he was driving.

Twelve years later, one December evening in 1955, Rosa left work and boarded a bus as usual, which, like all segregated buses, had three sections. The FRONT ten seats were for white passengers, the back ten seats were for black people, and the middle 16 seats were for anyone . . . but if a white passenger couldn't find a seat, any black passengers in the middle section had to give up theirs and move further back or stand. It was against the law for black and white people to sit in the same row. It may sound like some kind of crazy game, but it was no game.

Rosa sat where she was allowed, in the front of the middle section. But after a few stops, the front ten seats filled up. The rules were clear: the front section just got BIGGER, while the middle section shrank. One extra white passenger meant that FOUR sitting black passengers had to move rows.

Three passengers headed back as instructed, but when the driver told Rosa to move, she recognized him as James F. Blake, the driver she'd vowed to avoid. So Rosa refused. She'd had enough. "I instantly felt God give me the STRENGTH to endure whatever would happen next," Rosa later wrote. "God's PEACE flooded my soul, and my fear melted away. All people were equal in the eyes of God, and I was going to live like a free person."

Rosa was not the first to refuse to give up her seat. Nine months earlier, 15-year-old Claudette Colvin did the same – also on a bus in Montgomery – and she was arrested. Thirteen years earlier in 1942, activist Bayard Rustin boarded a bus from Kentucky to Tennessee; he smiled at a young white child, and then thought that if he carried on to the back seats, the child might think he was happy back there. So he sat illegally in the whites-only row, and was soon arrested and beaten. Or we could go back to 1841! Frederick Douglass refused to leave a train carriage reserved for white passengers, so a mob attacked him.

Throughout history, activists have stood up (or sat down) against injustice. Many have chosen peaceful means.

Here are a few non-violent notables:

The Conflict of Orders (494 BC): Working-class Roman citizens refused to work in protest at their wealthy (and very bossy) bosses, in one of the oldest known non-violent campaigns.

Peterloo (1819): Around 60,000 British people, "armed with no other weapon but that of a self-approving conscience", protested at unemployment. The government sent armed soldiers on horseback to attack the crowd.

Women's Suffrage Parade (1913): Five thousand American women marched on Washington, wanting the right to vote. With bullish crowds of men on either side, some protesters had to march in a single line to fit through the narrowing onlookers.

The Salt March (1930): Mahatma Gandhi led a long walk – over 240 miles – to collect just a handful of sea salt. This tiny act was illegal, as India's occupying British government banned locals from collecting salt, and resulted in over 60,000 arrests.

Black Lives Matter (2020): After African American George Floyd was killed by the police, vigils and demonstrations that were almost entirely peaceful took place across the world, highlighting racism in society.

Can you think of any more? No problem if you can't, just keep reading!

In Rosa's case, the bus driver called the police and she was **ARRESTED**. The bus went on its way, while Rosa sat in jail. In response, minister and civil rights activist Martin Luther King, Jr., along with other church leaders, began a campaign in her support. They would ask black passengers to boycott (refuse to ride) the Montgomery buses on the day Rosa was due in court.

That day, Rosa paid $14 to the court as a punishment, then went free . . . but the boycott went ahead and without any black passengers on the buses, the company lost money in sales.

The leaders decided to continue boycotting the buses until black people were treated **FAIRLY**. For over a year, many people found other ways to travel. Some

walked, others shared car rides, black taxi drivers reduced their fares for African Americans, and some white women drove their African American servants to work. The bus company lost a **LOT** of money!

And so it worked! The bus segregation laws were lifted, and all passengers could CHOOSE where to sit. Rosa boarded a bus again just before Christmas 1956 . . . to see the same bus driver again. "He didn't react," she said, "and neither did I."

The bus boycott was a **HUGE** moment for the civil rights movement, but it wasn't the end. Other places stayed segregated, and there were campaigns such as restaurant sit-ins, with black diners refusing to move seats, just as Rosa had. There were difficulties and *death threats*, and Rosa and Raymond didn't find life easy. For their own safety they moved away from the area to find new jobs.

Over 40 years after Rosa refused to give up her seat, she was awarded the Congressional Gold Medal: the **HIGHEST** award the President could give her. Rosa's brave act was a key moment in making the world a fairer place. Her faith in God was one of utter **TRUST**; she felt his presence as she faced off against the bus driver. A moment of *panic* turned into a moment of calm and defiance, that sent ripples around the city, the state, the country, and the planet.

"I LEARNED TO PUT MY TRUST IN GOD AND TO SEEK HIM AS MY STRENGTH."

ROSA PARKS

THINK

- How do you think Rosa felt when she looked up to see Blake the bus driver again? Was it a coincidence that she boarded his bus? Or do you think God planned for them to meet?

- Have you ever taken a stand against something that wasn't fair? How did it make you feel? Learn the Bible verse below, and next time you see someone being treated unfairly, or you're treated unfairly, calmly repeat it to yourself.

READ

Be strong and courageous. Do not be frightened, and do not be dismayed, for the LORD your God is with you wherever you go.

Joshua 1:9

PRAY

Our Lord and Protector,

Thank you for the brave, peaceful protesters who have come before us. Thank you for those who have stood up for what they believed in, not thinking of the cost to themselves. Thank you for Rosa Parks's life, faith, and great courage. Help us be brave, selfless, and loving, and give us a heart for justice, so that we can help make the world around us fairer and safer for everyone.

Amen.

CHAPTER 6

WANGARĨ MAATHAI

(1940–2011)

Sometimes changing the world is about changing attitudes to the world. After all, there's **NO PLANET B** . . . and we should save the Earth – it's the only planet with chocolate . . . and you might know other world-saving slogans. (Maybe you've even made up your own?)

This is the story of Professor Dr Wangarĩ Maathai: a Kenyan environmentalist, activist, feminist, politician . . . and the first African woman to win the world's most famous award for promoting FRIENDSHIP between nations, the Nobel Peace Prize!

It's also a story about a plane, a university that was more a zoo-niversity . . . and a tree. (You may not have seen a zoo-niversity before, but I bet you've seen a tree. This book was once part of one. Ooh, there's a thought. Better go and plant some new trees . . . It's what Wangarĩ would want.)

Wangarĩ Miriam Muta was born in 1940 in the village of Ihithe in the Kenyan highlands in East Africa. Her family were Christians and belonged to the Kikuyu ethnic group, which makes up about a quarter of the country's population.

At the time Kenya was governed by the British, and Wangarĩ's father worked as a chauffeur and a farmhand on white-owned land. Wangarĩ was the eldest daughter, so she helped her mother at home, especially enjoying the garden and the trees. Trees are so LOVELY, don't you think? (She did!)

Her brothers went to school, and one day they asked their mother why eight-year-old Wangarĩ stayed at home. Their mother agreed this wasn't fair, so that same week Wangarĩ started at the local school. It was the start of her life of EDUCATION.

Later, at a boarding school, Wangarĩ learned more about Christianity from Catholic nuns. Their humble, dedicated FAITH planted in her a desire to serve the community. There was more planting to come too, as she gained a love of nature in God's universe. With her family of rural farmers, she was very aware of the relationship between people and the land.

When Wangarĩ left school (**TOP** of her class!), she was given the opportunity to go to college in the United States and soon she was *flying* from Kenya to Kansas to continue her studies.

Wangarĩ earned two degrees in the United States, both in biology. During her time there, she lived with nuns who encouraged her love of SCIENCE, and became like family to her. She returned home for a job at the University College of Nairobi's zoology department.

But on arrival, the job had been given to a man! She believed that she was a victim of *prejudice* because of her tribe, and being female. Months later she found another job as a research assistant in the Veterinary Anatomy department, which studied animals' bodies. She also met and married Mwangi Mathai, giving her the surname Mathai, although when they divorced years later, she added another "a" to her name, making it Maathai, to mark that *change*. But she had titles to add to the front of her name, too . . .

In 1971, she became the **FIRST** East African woman to earn a doctorate degree: now she was a Doctor (but not the kind who looks at your tonsils) and six years later she

added yet another title to her name, becoming the country's FIRST female professor.

Wangarĩ kept thinking of Jesus' teaching: "Love others as yourself." This motivated her to find ways to HELP her fellow citizens. So in 1977 – the same year she became a professor – she began the Green Belt Movement. One focus was on caring for the environment and planting trees. But its other focus was on women's rights.

Wangarĩ had grown up among lush forests, but since her childhood THOUSANDS of trees had been cut down to make room for HUGE farms that grew wheat and tea. Wangarĩ could see that women were having to walk further than they used to in order to fetch water or wood for fuel. Rivers were drying up and it was difficult to grow crops. She thought that development should be sustainable, which means that we should only use the Earth's resources (like trees) in a way that protects them for our children and our children's children to enjoy.

The Green Belt Movement EDUCATED women about farming, teaching skills such as forestry and beekeeping, and enabled them to earn money by planting trees. Thousands of women were EMPOWERED to look after themselves and their families at the same time as looking after the environment. Everyone WON!

Wangarĩ soon noticed the challenges for those she was helping. The entire system was against them. Not just the environment, but politics, society, and business made life difficult for those working the land. Leaders had been greedy, making money and increasing their own power, rather than helping people. So her focus shifted.

She'd still encourage tree planting to help the poorest people, but now she'd also hold the powerful to account. Wangarĩ wanted to protect rainforests, teach farmers,

Wangarĩ told a traditional tale about a hummingbird:

There is a huge forest and a huge forest fire. The animals who live there look at the fire, transfixed, as it spreads and burns. They feel powerless.

But they notice a hummingbird flying back and forth above them. "I'm going to do something about the fire!" says the bird, flying off to the nearest stream, then back with a tiny drop of water. It deposits the droplet on the fire, then flies back to the stream for the next drop. Back and forth, as fast as it can.

The elephant stands below, motionless and helpless, with its huge trunk capable of holding so much water. "What do you think you can do?" the elephant says to the hummingbird. "You're too little!"

Other animals call up too: "Your wings are too small . . . Your beak's too tiny . . . Your wings will burn . . . The fire's too big . . . It's only a drop . . . "

Without missing a flap of its wings as it passes overhead, the hummingbird says: "I am doing the best I can."

Wangarĩ said that she had chosen to be that animal, as all of us should. "I will be a hummingbird. I will do the best I can."

encourage democracy, fight for women's rights, and so much more. It was all connected!

One time, when the Kenyan government wanted to build a HUGE skyscraper on a park in Nairobi, Wangarĩ led a protest against it . . . and won! Sometimes she was beaten, arrested, and jailed for her political activism. Those in power did not like her shining a spotlight on them.

Throughout, she linked her ecological work with the first book in the Bible. She asked her colleagues to read the Genesis creation account – how God looked at the Earth he'd created and said, "And that is GOOD." She wondered, if God were to look at today's troubled land and disappearing rivers, would he still say "This is good"? It was a challenge to her and others to match up to God's vision for the world.

Wangarĩ ran a campaign asking that each year on Easter Monday, we should plant a tree, marking the resurrection and new life of Easter. After all, Jesus died on a cross of wood and she believed that God provided salvation through that one tree, and therefore we should say thank you to every tree we pass. And if God used that for his plan, then we too should be planting trees and NURTURING nature in thanksgiving to God. "It's the little things citizens do," she wrote. "That's what will make the difference. My little thing is planting trees."

Wangarĩ was chair of the National Council of Women of Kenya from 1979 to 1987, and became a politician in 2002, winning a **WHOPPING** 98% of votes! She became Assistant Minister for Environment and Natural Resources, and was soon awarded the Nobel Peace Prize for her work in "sustainable development, democracy, and peace".

Today, the Green Belt Movement continues to plant trees and empower communities. It has planted over 51 million trees in Kenya and **MILLIONS** more across Africa. Wangarĩ dreamt of a changed world, if people could *shift* their attitude to the environment. "In a few decades," she said, "the relationship between the environment, resources and conflict may seem almost as obvious as the connection we see today between human rights, democracy and PEACE."

What do you think? Are we moving in the right direction?

"WHEN WE PLANT TREES,
WE PLANT THE SEEDS
OF PEACE AND HOPE."

WANGARĪ MAATHAI

THINK

- In the hummingbird story, the bird does what it can to extinguish the fire. What do you do in your average week to help look after God's world? What other things could you start or stop doing?

- Wangarĩ understood that nature is God's gift to all people, including those who aren't born yet. How might that understanding change the way we think and behave towards nature?

READ

And God saw everything that he had made, and behold, it was very good.

Genesis 1:31

PRAY

Creator God,

Please forgive us for the damage we have done to your world. Help us care for the plants, animals, and one other, and remind us of the connection between all living things. Thank you for Wangarĩ' Maathai's dedication in serving you and helping those around her. Help us care for those near and far, and those yet to come, who haven't walked your lovely planet. Help us to prepare it, to make it nice for them!

Amen.

CHAPTER 7

CHRISTIAN FÜHRER

(1943-2014)

Have you ever walked through a crowd where everyone else seems to be walking the other way? It feels **ODD** being the **one** person heading in the opposite direction. In a country where speaking out against the government could cost your freedom and even your life, our next world changer was not afraid to raise his **voice** . . . but he never raised his **fists**.

This is the story of Christian Führer: a German church pastor whose weekly "peace prayer" events were as regular as clockwork, turning prayer into **PEACEFUL** protest that brought change across Europe.

It's also a story about a prayer meeting, the police, and the Berlin Wall. The Berlin Wall wasn't just **any** old wall. It was one of the most important walls in the world. Think of a famous wall. **NO**, it was more important than that. Even more importantly, it's no longer standing. To find out why, let's meet Christian . . .

Christian was born in 1943 in Leipzig, Germany, in the middle of the Second World War. He was two years old when the war ended, and Germany was divided into West and East Germany. Christian was in East Germany, occupied by the Soviet Union.

Life wasn't easy in East Germany. The communist leaders DIDN'T like opposition. In 1953, when workers demonstrated against their conditions in various East German cities, soldiers opened fire on protesters. The people went back to struggling with their daily lives –

The Union of Soviet Socialist Republics (USSR), or Soviet Union, was the largest country that ever existed (nearly two and half times the size of the United States). It had 15 republics, or states, the largest of which was what we now call Russia.

The republics in the USSR were all communist. This means that instead of individual people owning property, like land and factories, they were owned by the government or the community and everyone shared the wealth.

This might sound like a good idea, but in practice it didn't really work. Only a few people ended up with power and money, and most people lost most of their freedoms, including the right to vote freely.

lives of hard work, low standards of living, and not much hope.

Christian had little hope in East Germany's human leaders, but he had GREAT hope in God. He became pastor of a church, to pass on that message of hope to others.

In 1980, in a time of great tension between East and West, Christian become the pastor of *Nikolaikirche* – St Nicholas's church – in Leipzig. It was a difficult country to be a Christian in, as religion was pretty much banned. The government enforced "state atheism" and hugely discouraged belief in God.

Any form of dissent – that is, speaking against the government – wasn't tolerated. In the 1950s and 1960s, those who spoke out were often arrested. By the 1970s and 1980s, there weren't so many arrests and instead the government tried to unsettle its enemies, which included Christians. Some had workplace gossip spread about them, or received mysterious phone calls, or even had their homes broken into with nothing stolen but pictures moved, or one type of tea swapped for another! If you came home to find your socks had moved drawers, it was the government trying to make you confused.

In 1982, seeing the need for HOPE in the city around him, Christian opened the church for those who wanted to share their frustrations and concerns about the government's actions. With the government so nervous of protest, it was RISKY. More people turned up than were expected, mostly young people. Christian had them sit on the floor around a large flat cross. They didn't dare speak, until Christian encouraged them to light a candle, place it by the cross and say what was on their mind. The more people spoke, the more the cross was ILLUMINATED in peaceful light.

The young pray-ers returned week after week, every
Monday at 5 p.m. for what Christian called "peace prayers".
They spoke of FREED0M, and they spoke more freely
here than anywhere else, even in their own homes, as many
were paranoid they might be heard. The church seemed to
offer some protection.

In 1987 Christian arranged a PEACE march, and
held prayers for protesters who had been arrested. He
began speaking out more politically, yet still carefully and
peacefully.

After the Second World War, Germany's capital city Berlin was divided into four, each area controlled by a different country: the United States, Britain, France, and the Soviet Union.

The first three countries united to form West Berlin, but the Soviet Union side became East Berlin.

Life was difficult in communist East Berlin (and East Germany), so many people left for a new life in West Berlin (and West Germany). In the 1950s, over 2 million people fled East to West.

This risked making the country unstable and embarrassed the communist government, because if communism was so good, why would so many want to flee? So to keep East Germans in, the Berlin Wall was built in 1961.

The heavily guarded concrete wall stretched for 27 miles. Over 100,000 people tried to escape over it, some succeeded and some died trying.

But the wall isn't up now. So how did the wall fall down? Christian played a part . . .

In 1989, Monday's peace prayers gained a **LOT** more people. The wind of change was *blowing* through the Soviet Union. Some states changed leadership and opened borders, bringing whispers of hope for the East German people, and worry for those in charge. People who were previously afraid to attend the prayer meetings now tiptoed out of their homes and joined them.

The church **OVERFLOWED** with peace pray-ers, so latecomers, holding candles, had to stand outside on the street. It was a small step from standing on the street to *marching* on the street.

Towards the end of 1989, the marches grew from a few hundred people, to a few thousand, and then to a few **HUNDRED THOUSAND** people marching across the land, led in Leipzig by Christian. Peace prayers had become public protest, people wanted FREEDOM and DEMOCRACY. Christian urged them to avoid violence.

The police threatened the marchers and beat and arrested some at *random*, but the protestors resisted violence. Christian's encouragement and faith had given them CONFIDENCE.

The authorities were worried about the power of Christian's peaceful gathering at his church the following Monday. So **8,000** armed police and soldiers were sent to stop the demonstrations . . . with **FORCE** if necessary. Local hospitals were told to prepare extra beds, in readiness for a *dangerous* clash.

Not only that, but hundreds of members of the secret police (and other government loyalists) arrived early at the church to stop the usual prayer meeting from happening. They'd taken up **ALL** the seats!

Christian used this as a chance to preach to them! He read the Sermon on the Mount and begged them to be peaceful as they left. When the seat-blocking government supporters left the church, they found tens of thousands of candle-holding PEACEFUL protesters outside. In all, **70,000** people showed up that Monday! They marched, chanting "We are the people!" as armed police looked on.

As each protester held tightly to their prayer candle with one hand, and sheltered it from the breeze with their other hand, **NO** stone was thrown and **NO** fist was raised in anger. Faced with a peaceful protest, local politicians ordered the guards to stand down. This day was called "the beginning of the end" of East Germany. One government member later told how peace beat violence that day: "We were prepared for everything – but not candles and prayers."

The protests continued, joined by **HALF A MILLION** people throughout East Germany. Nine days later, the

East German leader resigned. The citizens were no longer afraid – they were on the MOVE. Some tried heading to countries to the west. Countless East Germans gathered near newly opened border crossings.

To ease the squeeze, the government announced that movement from East to West would finally be allowed. In Berlin, the trouble was there was a wall in the way . . .

HUGE crowds gathered by the Berlin Wall. After many panicked phone calls from border guards, the checkpoints were opened, allowing FREE movement. West Germans greeted East Germans and chunks of the wall were knocked down in CELEBRATION. The two countries began to be unified as one in what became known as the Peaceful Revolution. Just over two years later, the Soviet Union itself CRUMBLED.

Christian's surname "Führer" simply means "leader", so he was literally named "Christian Leader" and he fully lived up to this! Once Germany was unified, he championed the unemployed, founding Leipzig's Church Initiative for the Jobless. He also continued with the peace prayers, even in times of political calm. He believed in the POWER OF PRAYER in the world. In his case, those prayers were WALL-TOPPLING and world changing.

"PRAYERS PREVENTED US FROM DROWNING IN FEAR AND GAVE US STRENGTH."

CHRISTIAN FÜHRER

THINK

- Prayer can be by yourself or with others. How do you feel when you pray? How might praying with other people, perhaps at church, feel different to praying by yourself?

- Christian trusted in the power of prayer. Sometimes there are worrying problems in the world that it is impossible for one person to fix. If there's something worrying you, bring the problem to God in prayer and trust him with the outcome.

READ

The LORD is near to all who call on him,
to all who call on him in truth.

Psalm 145:18

PRAY

God of peace,

Thank you for Christian Führer and peaceful leaders like him, and bless those today who stand up for unity, peace, and hope. We pray for all people who are suffering because of war and for those who live in countries where the government oppresses them. All-powerful God, we thank you that you hear your people's prayers in their time of need. May you comfort and strengthen them.

Amen.

CHAPTER 8

JONI EARECKSON TADA

(1949–)

What do you want to be when you're older? An athlete? A singer? A radio presenter? An artist? A businessperson? Oh, and a world changer, of course . . . Sometimes you can head towards your goal but BUMP into a brick wall. A dead end? Nah. Maybe it's just telling you to try a different direction. (Oh, and I'm 45 and STILL haven't decided what to be when I'm older . . .)

This is the story of Joni Eareckson Tada: an American author, artist, activist . . . and those are only her jobs beginning with the letter A! Before becoming a world changer herself, Joni dealt with her whole world being changed, facing this with FAITH and COURAGE, and finding a new purpose.

It's also a story about a dive, a painting, and a wheelchair. Well, lots of wheelchairs . . . upcycled!

Joni was born in 1949 in Baltimore, Maryland, into a sporty family. Her father, John, was an Olympic wrestler, while her mother, Lindy, loved athletics. Joni grew up in a world of swimming, tennis, and riding horses. When Joni was just four, the family *enjoyed* a hundred-mile horse-ride! (I say "enjoyed" . . .)

But Joni's world *changed* in the summer of 1967, when she went swimming in nearby Chesapeake Bay. She positioned herself to dive into the water and took the plunge, but the sea was not as deep as she thought. She hit the surface with a horrid *THUD*.

Joni was saved by both her sister and the tide, *pulling* and *pushing* her when she couldn't move out of the water. The collision was particularly nasty, breaking Joni's neck. She was 17 years old and paralyzed, unable to move from the shoulders down.

Joni spent months in hospital lying flat but eventually was able to sit in a wheelchair and go home. She'd had a firm FAITH since childhood but at times she felt frustrated and depressed by her limitations.

Joni overcame those feelings with a **CAN-DO** attitude. She loved painting . . . but how to paint when she couldn't move her arms or legs? She was taught to paint by clutching a paintbrush between her teeth. After lots of practice

and hard work, Joni went on to paint such **IMPRESSIVE** pictures, many themed on Bible stories, that people wanted to buy them.

Joni was eager to help those facing similar challenges. But as we **ALL** face limitations, disappointments, and doubts, Joni's story spoke to many people, whether they'd had similar experiences or not.

In 1976, using a wand pen in her mouth, Joni wrote her first book. It was the story of her life, and its main message was not tragedy and despair but HOPE! It became an international bestseller and four years later it was adapted as a film. Joni played herself.

In 1979 she began her radio show, *Joni and Friends*, to bring Christian ministry to the disability community. It's still on the air today! She was PASSIONATE to spread her positive message.

But there was more to do. To HELP those in times of crisis, Joni and Friends became a charitable organization campaigning, speaking, running getaway camps for families affected by disability, and much more.

There were barriers EVERYWHERE in society, though. Joni helped to tackle the problem from the top when she was appointed to the National Council on Disability by American President Ronald Reagan. The council helped write the Americans with Disabilities Act, which gave a whole list of ways to make life FAIRER for people with disabilities. Joni was at the White House, the home and office of the American President, when the Act was signed into law.

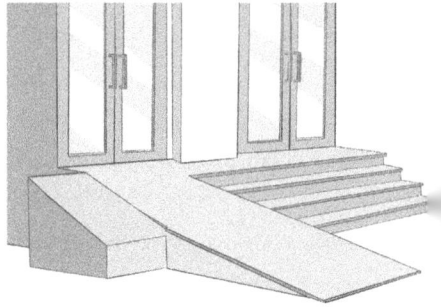

A change in law was a start, but there was MUCH work still to do. As Joni wrote: "If access is having a ramp to the table, mainstreaming is having a seat at the table, and inclusion is having a voice at the table, then true embrace is being heard at the table." Joni and Friends continues working towards CHANGING HEARTS.

At church, Joni had met history teacher Ken Tada, and they had fallen in love and married. Ken helped Joni have a music career in a rather unusual way. As well as the radio, books, and artwork, Joni released an album of songs. But her lungs couldn't fit enough air to hit the high notes. So during the recording, Ken pushed her diaphragm in time with the music, giving her more breath and increasing her range.

As Joni embarked on speaking tours, she noticed a lack of resources for people with disabilities. There might be ramps at a church, but not enough wheelchairs for those who wanted to come!

It used to be easy for public places such as restaurants and shops to say "no" to people with additional needs. Joni herself had been refused entry to venues because of her wheelchair, and she'd seen others find it difficult to get jobs or housing.

Despite practical reasons why some buildings might not accommodate wheelchairs, or certain jobs might be tricky to adapt, this widespread refusal to meet the needs of people with disabilities amounted to one thing: discrimination.

When the Americans with Disabilities Act became law, the United States became the first country in the world to make it illegal to discriminate against someone because of a disability. The changes it required included:

- mechanical lifts on buses,
- elevator buttons labelled in Braille (a written language for blind people),
- ramps at entrances to libraries or museums,
- service dogs allowed in music venues,
- closed-caption subtitles on TV shows, for the hard of hearing,
- support in school for children with autism.

The Act changed lives for the better, not only in America but also in the rest of the world: other countries began to introduce similar laws, including Australia in 1992 and the UK in 1995.

So Joni and Friends started Wheels for the World, an organization collecting wheelchairs and mobility devices, then refurbishing them for future use. Often the restoration work was done in prison workshops, then the chairs might be sent overseas or to churches across the country. This allowed MORE people with access needs to get around and feel more VALUED in society.

Joni was once asked if there are wheelchairs in heaven and she wasn't sure. On the one hand, she DIDN'T like the need for a wheelchair, and liked to think that she'd see the

last of it by the time she gets to heaven! On the other hand, her wheelchair was a GIFT from God, a core part of her story. Besides, in the book of Daniel in the Bible, it says: "Thrones were placed, and the Ancient of Days took his seat . . . his throne was fiery flames, its wheels were BURNING fire." Sounds like a wheelchair to me!

Joni imagined her heavenly wheelchair encrusted with jewels and gilded with gold . . . upcycling up there, too! She looked forward to a NEW BODY in heaven, so she could get down on new knees and thank the Lord for working through our sufferings.

Joni shared the GOOD NEWS of Jesus to people EVERYWHERE. As well as speaking to large crowds, sometimes to 100,000 people, she's written around 50 books, including some for children, and almost all of them tell her inspirational tale of hope in suffering. Joni has often spoken of RESILIENCE – being able to bounce back after tough times – something she needed again in recent years when she faced cancer, twice.

Joni is a world changer who has always aimed HIGH – from the White House to her songs' high notes! Her positive outlook after a major crisis in her life has brought changes to the law, changes in attitudes, and changes of faith as her listeners put their TRUST in God.

"I'D RATHER BE IN THIS WHEELCHAIR KNOWING GOD THAN ON MY FEET WITHOUT HIM."

JONI EARECKSON TADA

THINK

- Joni found life hard after her accident, but positive things came from it. Think of something that happened to you – or to a friend – that seemed bad. Can you think of something positive that came from it, even if it took a while?

- What do you want to be when you're older? Maybe ask God what he wants you to be too! Where might he put you in the world? And whose world might you change for the better?

READ

And we know that for those who love God all things work together for good, for those who are called according to his purpose.

Romans 8:28

PRAY

Healing Father,

Thank you for Joni Eareckson Tada's courage and dedication, at a time when she could so easily have given up hope. We pray for all who suffer medical problems, especially those who feel limited, lost or isolated. Thank you that whatever happens in our lives, we can put our trust in you and know that your love for us will never end.

Amen.

FANTASTICALLY FAITHFUL FINAL THOUGHTS

Well then! Those are our eight incredible tales from eight incredible people. But amazingly, they weren't born special. They were no more special than you and me (although in God's eyes we're ALL special, aren't we).

None of them set out at the start of their lives to do anything so grand as change the entire world. They didn't have positions of great power; instead many of them had everyday jobs and hobbies: sailor, seamstress, student, swimmer. Some of them seemingly had nothing much in life, from sleeping on hay to being denied a bus seat.

But then what did they experience? A storm, a diving accident, a moment of extreme prejudice. They met prisoners or orphans, saw drying rivers or deadly clashes with government. They farmed, taught, preached, prayed, stood UP for what mattered, sat down for what mattered . . .

. . . and God saw that they were GOOD!

But with change came *challenge*. None of them found their chosen path easy. They've been arrested and jailed, often wrongly. They faced prejudice, bullies, and powerful leaders who wanted them to stop.

Our world changers dug *deep*. (Wangarĩ kept digging deep, and planting more trees!) They leaned on God, prayed a **LOT**, and stayed focused.

The world's problems are surely too **BIG** for one person to fix. But each of these fantastically faithful world changers picked a problem and improved what they could. Joni saw that disability rights needed reforming. John saw the horrors of slavery. Thomas housed London's orphans. Rosa saw that if you can't sit where you like on a bus . . . *you're* not wrong, the *system* is.

Here's another thing many of them did: they **CREATED**! John kept writing songs, eventually "Amazing Grace". Wangarĩ told stories of hummingbirds and other animals. George painted pictures of nature. Joni painted with her mouth!

Whatever **YOU** do to change the world, keep creating, singing, laughing, playing, designing, inventing . . . and trusting.

God's got this. God's got you. So **YOU GOT THIS**.

Finally then, a blessing for you, wherever you are with this book in hand. Because in a moment, you'll put it down, and do something else. Maybe sleep. Maybe plan. Maybe do. So whatever God's got in store for you . . .

May the faith of John Newton,
the care of Elizabeth Fry,
the kindness of Thomas Barnardo,
the dedication of George Washington Carver,
the justice of Rosa Parks,
the natural curiosity of Wangarĩ Maathai,
the bravery of Christian Führer,
the positivity of Joni Eareckson Tada,
and the wonder of you
be yours this day and throughout your lifetime,
and the blessing of God almighty,
the Father, the Son, and the Holy Spirit,
be among you and remain with you always.
Amen.

(If you've read *Fantastically Faithful Heroes Who Gave their All for God*, you'll know why I've written my prayer for you like this. If you haven't read it yet . . . well, rush out and get it, and be inspired by some heroes.)

I've loved bringing these tales to you. They're all TRUE, and they're all yours now, to tell others, if you like. And maybe one day we'll add your tale of how **YOU** changed the world? That would be cool.

Whatever your hopes and plans, whatever challenges God has ahead for you, I pray that your decisions and actions will help CHANGE THE WORLD for the better (even the **small** decisions – especially the small decisions?).

Shall we start tomorrow? Or how about **TODAY**?

ACKNOWLEDGEMENTS

p. 13: John Newton quotation taken from https://scriptoriumdaily.com/john-newton-accidentally-called-out-for-mercy/ (accessed January 2025)

p. 18: "Amazing Grace", *Olney Hymns*, John Newton, 1779

p. 27: Elizabeth Fry quotation taken from https://www.biblesociety.org.uk/latest/news/the-angel-of-prisons/ (accessed January 2025)

p. 30: Elizabeth Fry quotation taken from *Memoir of the Life of Elizabeth Fry*, C. Gilpin and J. Hatchard, 1847

p. 35–36: Thomas Barnardo quotation taken from https://www.childrenshomes.org.uk/JimJarvis/#:~:text=I%20looked%20at%20the%20little,he%20must%20have%20suffered!' (accessed January 2025)

p. 41: Thomas Barnardo quotation taken from https://upload.wikimedia.org/wikipedia/commons/1/1e/Memorial_to_Dr_Barnardo.jpg (accessed January 2025)

p. 45: George Washington Carver quotation taken from https://en.wikipedia.org/wiki/George_Washington_Carver#Christianity (accessed January 2025)

p. 46: Mariah Watkins quotation taken from *George Washington Carver: The Man Who Overcame*, L. Elliott, 1971, p. 34

p. 47: George Washington Carver quotation taken from his letter to Hubert W. Pelt, dated February 1930

p. 50: George Washington Carver quotation taken from https://www.cslewisinstitute.org/resources/george-washington-carver-1860-1943/ (accessed January 2025)

p. 51: Inscription from George Washington Carver's gravestone taken from https://www.ncei.noaa.gov/news/legacy-dr-george-washington-carver (accessed January 2025)

p. 53: George Washington Carver quotation taken from https://www.cslewisinstitute.org/resources/george-washington-carver-1860-1943/ (accessed January 2025)

p. 57: Rosa Parks quotation taken from https://en.wikiquote.org/wiki/Rosa_Parks (accessed January 2025)

p. 58: Rosa Parks quotation taken from https://www.frc.org/blog/2021/03/rosa-parks-woman-quiet-strength-and-faith-who-galvanized-civil-rights-movement (accessed January 2025)

p. 64: Rosa Parks quotation taken from https://www.frc.org/blog/2021/03/rosa-parks-woman-quiet-strength-and-faith-who-galvanized-civil-rights-movement (accessed January 2025)

p. 72: Hummingbird story taken from https://www.google.com/search?q=wangari+maathai+hummingbird&rlz=1C1CHBF_en-GBGB999GB999&oq=wangari+maathai+hummingbird&gs_lcrp=EgZjaHJvbWUqCQgAEEU-YOxiABDIJCAAQRRg7GIAEMgcIARAAGIAEMggIAhAAGBYYHjINCAMQABiGAxiABBiKBTINCAQ-QABiGAxiABBiKBTINCAUQABiGAxiABBiKBTI (accessed January 2025)

p. 73: Wangarĩ Maathai quotation taken from https://www.greenbeltmovement.org/node/345 (accessed January 2025)

p. 75: Wangarĩ Maathai quotation taken from https://unfoundation.org/blog/post/12-quotes-to-inspire-climate-action/ (accessed January 2025)

p. 76: Wangarĩ Maathai quotation taken from https://www.holytroublemakers.com/wangari (accessed January 2025)

p. 86: Government minister quotation taken from https://pres-outlook.org/2009/04/east-german-revolution-remembered-in-church-campaign/ (accessed January 2025)

p. 89: Christian Führer quotation taken from https://www.pbs.org/wnet/religionandethics/2009/11/06/

november-6-2009-the-rev-christian-fuhrer-extended-interview/4843/ (accessed January 2025)

p. 96: Joni Eareckson Tada quotation taken from https://joniandfriends.org/from-our-founder/did-the-americans-with-disabilities-act-really-guarantee-change/ (accessed January 2025)

p. 100: Joni Eareckson Tada quotation taken from The Case for Faith, Student Edition, Lee Strobel with Jane Vogel, 2014, p. 14

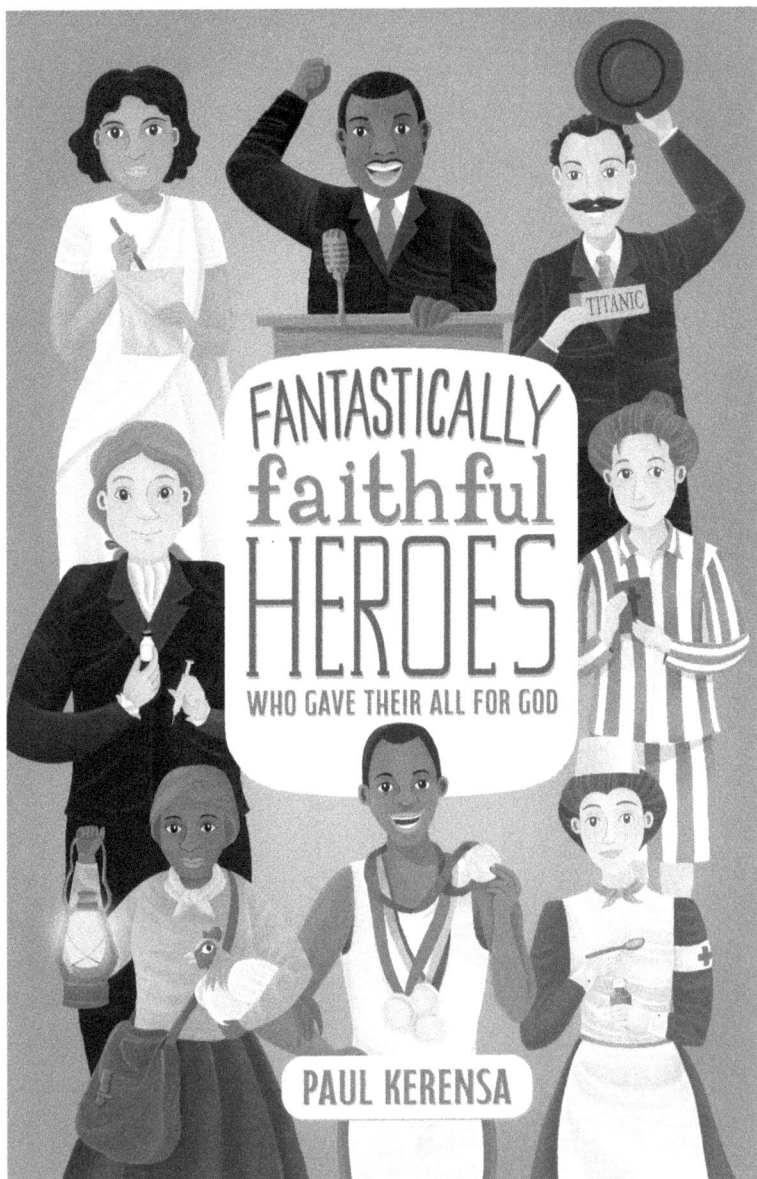

FANTASTICALLY faithful HEROES

WHO GAVE THEIR ALL FOR GOD

PAUL KERENSA